Hello _ _

My Old Friend

Sue Wilding

A SAMUEL FRENCH ACTING EDITION

FOUNDED 1830

SAMUELFRENCH.COM
SAMUELFRENCH-LONDON.CO.UK

FOR PRODUCTION ENQUIRIES

UNITED STATES AND CANADA

Info@SamuelFrench.com
1-866-598-8449

UNITED KINGDOM AND EUROPE

Plays@SamuelFrench-London.co.uk
020-7255-4302

Each title is subject to availability from Samuel French, depending upon country of performance. Please be aware that *HELLO DARKNESS MY OLD FRIEND* may not be licensed by Samuel French in your territory. Professional and amateur producers should contact the nearest Samuel French office or licensing partner to verify availability.

MUSIC USE NOTE

Licensees are solely responsible for obtaining formal written permission from copyright owners to use copyrighted music in the performance of this play and are strongly cautioned to do so. If no such permission is obtained by the licensee, then the licensee must use only original music that the licensee owns and controls. Licensees are solely responsible and liable for all music clearances and shall indemnify the copyright owners of the play(s) and their licensing agent, Samuel French, against any costs, expenses, losses and liabilities arising from the use of music by licensees. Please contact the appropriate music licensing authority in your territory for the rights to any incidental music.

IMPORTANT BILLING AND CREDIT REQUIREMENTS

If you have obtained performance rights to this title, please refer to your licensing agreement for important billing and credit requirements.

HELLO DARKNESS MY OLD FRIEND was first produced at Sedgefield Drama Festival in September 2009. The performance was directed by Sue Wilding. The cast was as follows:

PHIL . . . . David Irwin
SARAH. . . . . Shari Gledhill
JOE . . . . John Connor Halkyard

Winner of runner-up Best Production award, and
Best Performance by an Actor Under 18

Subsequently produced at Saltburn Drama Festival in March 2013. The performance was directed by Sue Wilding. The cast was as follows:

PHIL . . . . David Irwin
SARAH. . . . . .Rae Yaldren
JOE . . . . Will Stanway

Winner of Best Actor award, and the Adjudicator's Award

CHARACTERS

PHIL, middle-aged
SARAH, his ex-wife
JOE, 13 – 15, their son

SETTING

A bench in a quiet corner of a park

HELLO DARKNESS MY OLD FRIEND

(Scene: a quiet corner of a park. A bench, surrounded by bushes.)

(Music starts in black.)

(Lights up slowly.)

(A football rolls onto the stage from left, followed after a few seconds by **JOE**, *aged 13 – 15. He stops the ball with his foot and idly kicks it around as music plays, then kicks it into the wings, stage right, and runs off after it.)*

*(***PHIL** *enters from left. He is a middle-aged man, and he looks weary and run-down. He wanders around for a while, looking at the bushes, before he tentatively sits on the bench, looking straight ahead.)*

*(***JOE** *enters, holding the football. He stops when he sees* **PHIL**. *After a moment he sits on the bench next to him. They sit side by side for a moment, until* **PHIL** *senses his presence, closing his eyes in relief – at last,* **JOE** *has come to him.)*

(Music fades.)

PHIL. *(calmly)* And where have you been?

*(***JOE** *says nothing.)*

Joe, how many times have I told you about playing in this park?

*(***JOE** *shrugs.)*

Who did you come down here with?

(Still no response from **JOE**.*)*

PHIL. Who did you come down here with?

7

JOE. I'm only playing football.

PHIL. But you're not, are you?

> (*pause*)

> How long have you been here?

JOE. Dunno.

PHIL. Oh, don't start all that grumpy stuff with me, Joe. How long?

JOE. I told you! I don't know!

PHIL. You 'lost track of time'.

JOE. Yeah.

PHIL. And look what's happened.

JOE. Dad! Don't go on at me!

> (*JOE stands and starts sulkily rolling the ball around with his foot. For a moment, PHIL watches JOE with the ball.*)

PHIL. Your mum's been worried sick.

> (*JOE does not respond.*)

PHIL. Joe!

JOE. I heard you.

> (*pause*)

> Did she look for me?

PHIL. When?

JOE. After I left the house. Did she look for me? I bet she didn't.

PHIL. She didn't know you were missing.

JOE. And why was that?

PHIL. Joe, you left the—

JOE. – why was it?

PHIL. You left the—

JOE. – why didn't she know I was missing, Dad?

PHIL. You left the house without telling her.

JOE. Yeah? So?

PHIL. And your mum – well, she was getting ready to go out – it never occurred to her to look in your room. Why would she?

JOE. To make sure I was there? To make sure I was alright?

PHIL. Oh, come on. You know that never works. What happens when you shut yourself in your room? Your mum and me, we've shouted ourselves hoarse since you were about seven years old, trying to get you to answer.

JOE. Well, Mum doesn't do that any more. She's not interested in me now. Not since Glenda moved in. She doesn't care about you any more, Dad. And she doesn't care about me.

PHIL. Look—

JOE. – and before you start, I don't want to hear the speech.

PHIL. It wasn't a speech. We meant every word. Your mum and me, we might not be together any more, but nothing will—

JOE. – hang on. I know this song. "But nothing will change for you, Joe, we'll always love you and whatever happens, you'll come first with us." Load of bollocks.

PHIL. Oy.

JOE. Load of bollocks.

PHIL. It wasn't!

JOE. Do I come first with you then, Dad?

PHIL. Of course you—

JOE. – do I come first with Mum?

PHIL. Of course you do!

(pause)

JOE. Okay then, let's see. With Mum it's him first. Then the house. The gym. Her friends, then maybe me. Fifth on the list. With you I might be fourth. After your job, your car, and the internet.

(He smiles knowingly at **PHIL**.*)*

I know you're looking for a new woman, Dad. I've seen the sites you've been on. Mum's only just kicked you out, and you're already pawing the ground looking for somebody else.

(pause)

PHIL. *(indignant but amused)* Pawing the ground?

(JOE *smiles reluctantly.*)

And you think that's more important than you.

(JOE *defiantly bounces the ball, kicks it away from* PHIL *and follows it.* PHIL *watches him for a moment, eventually smiling.*)

You and that bloody ball. It's been on the end of your foot since you were about two.

JOE. *(thawing slightly)* Remember when I broke that window at Nan's?

PHIL. Remember?! Your nan's only just started speaking to me again.

JOE. It was a good shot, though.

PHIL. It was a great shot. I said so at the time. And that's why your nan stopped speaking to me.

JOE. What about that plastic dog turd we put in her washing up bowl?

PHIL. Er...we? You put it there.

JOE. But you bought it for me.

PHIL. *(mock serious)* Joseph Patrick Adamson. I would never have bought you a fake dog turd if I'd known you were going to put it in your grandmother's washing up bowl.

JOE. You wanted me to put it in her bed!

PHIL. That is beside the point.

(*They are both laughing now. Relaxing slightly,* JOE *picks up the ball and goes to sit with* PHIL *as he is speaking.*)

God, she screamed the place down, didn't she?

JOE. She was having a go at Grandad for not doing the washing up, and then she saw the turd in the bowl.

PHIL. For a second, I think she thought your grandad had done it.

JOE. Eeeuww! Dad!

(Pause. Anxious to talk, worried that JOE *might disappear again,* PHIL *leaps in.)*

PHIL. When you fall in love with a woman, Joe, you think—

JOE. – aw, no! Dad!—

PHIL. – when you fall in love with a woman, you think that's it. You think nothing will ever be better than this.

JOE. Don't start talking about sex. You'll freak me out.

PHIL. It's got nothing to do with – let me finish. It's got nothing to do with sex.

JOE. Course it is. Your generation's sex mad.

PHIL. *(insistent)* You find the woman, you think nothing will ever be better than this. And then you have a child. People will try and tell you it's a different kind of love, Joe, but it's not.

(He pauses to look at JOE, *who is unresponsive.)*

Remember when you used to run up behind me and jump onto my back? All the time, you did that. I'd be walking down the garden, or up the stairs, and suddenly, there you were, leaping onto me with your arms round my neck.

JOE. Dad. I was, like, two years old when I did that.

PHIL. Yeah. And the rest.

*(*JOE *smiles slightly.)*

The feeling I once had every time I watched your mum walk into a room…well, it was the same feeling I got whenever you did that big leap onto me. Or whenever I saw you running across a football field. It's like a big balloon. Here. Inside you. And every time you think it can't get any bigger, it does, and it's hard to breathe.

But here's the difference, Joe. Here's the thing I need you to understand. With a woman, it goes away. That magic, that fascination. It – dissipates. It gets lost in all the stuff. It becomes other things. If you're lucky, it becomes deeper things, better things. If not...well, you're screwed. But with your child...with your child, that feeling is as fresh and new every day as it was the first time you touched their hand. You would throw yourself under a speeding car to spare their pain. I can't expect you to understand that, but that's how it is.

(**PHIL** *is so relieved at having said what he wants to say, he sits back, smiling. But* **JOE** *is staring at him.*)

JOE. A speeding car?

PHIL. Yeah.

(**JOE** *stands up, shaking his head in disgust.*)

What?

(**JOE** *starts bouncing the football with great concentration.*)

Joe! What?... Talk to me!

(**PHIL** *gets up and grabs the ball.*)

Talk to me, Joe.

JOE. Why should I?

PHIL. Because I've tried to tell you how it is.

JOE. So you'd throw yourself under a speeding car to spare me any pain, right?

PHIL. Right.

JOE. You'd throw yourself under a speeding car. But you won't put what I want before what you want.

PHIL. Of course we will!

JOE. You and Mum don't live together any more! You think I wanted that?

PHIL. That's what I'm trying to say! Everything that's happened with your mum and me, our feelings for you haven't changed!

JOE. She's in the house and you're in a shitty flat above a betting shop—

PHIL. – not for long, though! Once we sort out the finances, I can—

JOE. – you're in a shitty flat above a betting shop, because you gave up without a fight. And because Mum thought more about shagging that knobhead Glenda than she did about me.

PHIL. Oy. You don't speak about your mother like that.

JOE. Why not? Have you never thought it?

PHIL. No.

JOE. Yes.

PHIL. But I'm allowed to. You're not.

(pause)

JOE. Why did you never tell me that football field thing? That balloon thing? Why have you waited till now?

PHIL. I wanted you to know!

JOE. But why now? And how did you know I'd be here?

PHIL. I didn't!

JOE. You shoved me away, Dad! Both of you shoved me away. You were both like "go up to your room, Joe" when you wanted to have a row. "I'm moving out because I can't hack it, Joe, but here's a new iPod". And she's like "I can't come to your school play, Joe – it's Glenn's office party and I have to be there". And you sat back and let it happen, because you're a dickhead.

(He reaches for his football, and PHIL holds it out of reach.)

Give me the ball, Dad.

PHIL. No.

JOE. Give me it.

PHIL. No! I want to talk.

JOE. Give me the ball! You were quick enough to shove it into my hands to keep me quiet while you were surfing the net for a new woman! It's too late to talk now!

(He takes the ball and goes to exit.)

PHIL. Joe! Wait!

JOE. Too late, Dad!

PHIL. When are you coming back?

*(**JOE** has gone.)*

Joe!

*(**PHIL** watches the exit helplessly. After a moment, his wife **SARAH** enters. **PHIL** does not see her, and she stands watching him for a moment. He finally senses her presence.)*

PHIL. Don't start.

SARAH. Phil, we've talked about this.

PHIL. I came to look for Joe.

SARAH. What good can this possibly do?

(pause)

PHIL. So where's Glenn? At the gym, I suppose. Wouldn't do to neglect the old pecs, would it?

SARAH. Glenn didn't think this concerned him.

PHIL. Glenn didn't think this concerned him? Joe's your child! Of course it concerns him! Of course it bloody well – if you go into a relationship where there's a child involved, you can't pretend that child doesn't exist!

SARAH. Make your mind up! One minute you're telling me to keep Glenn out of anything to do with Joe, and now you're telling me he should be involved.

PHIL. Let's have a chat about why Joe disappeared.

(Pause. They have obviously had this argument before.)

SARAH. So you're saying I shouldn't be allowed a life of my own.

PHIL. Not at Joe's expense. He felt sidelined.

SARAH. In your opinion.

PHIL. Not just mine.

SARAH. Phil...

PHIL. Putting your slap on to go out, tarting yourself up, when you should have been checking up on him.

SARAH. Alright, that's enough. You know as well as I do what Joe's been like for the last few years. An earthquake wouldn't get him out of his room. And that evening... that evening, I behaved exactly as I would have if you'd still been living there. For God's sake.

*(Pause. **PHIL** knows that **SARAH** is right.)*

PHIL. *(sadly)* It was my rule, wasn't it?

SARAH. *(trying to be kind)* It was your rule. It was a good rule.

PHIL. I told him we wouldn't keep trying to coax him out of his room. If he was late for school, it was down to him. If he missed a meal, tough.

SARAH. It was a good rule.

PHIL. *(helplessly)* I was only trying to make him take some responsibility.

SARAH. Oh, Phil. You weren't to know he'd just decide to take off like that.

*(Pause. **PHIL** goes back on the attack.)*

PHIL. Of course, if we'd still been together—

SARAH. – oh Phil, no—

PHIL. – if we'd still been together—

SARAH. – not this again—

PHIL. – if we'd still been together – listen to me. Joe wouldn't have felt the need to run off. He felt neglected.

SARAH. He wasn't neglected.

PHIL. I said he felt neglected. He felt that Glenn was more important to you than he was.

SARAH. He told you that, did he?

PHIL. Yes.

SARAH. When?

(pause)

I told Joe I loved him every day.

PHIL. Oh, did you? You told Joe you loved him every day. Well, hooray for Hollywood. You did everything right.

SARAH. I never claimed to—

PHIL. – you did everything right. It's all boxed off. You told him you loved him, so now you can just move forward and get over it.

(pause)

SARAH. *(quietly)* Get over it? Get over it? You think I'm even close to getting over it? Shame on you. Shame on you, you self-indulgent shit.

(Pause. PHIL is ashamed, but won't apologise.)

So come on then. Dad of the Year. Did you ever tell him you loved him?

PHIL. *(not wanting to hear it)* We put our own needs before his.

SARAH. Did you ever tell him you loved him?

PHIL. Our marriage de-railed, and Joe got shunted into a siding. Because he'd still be there, wouldn't he? He'd be there waiting. When we'd sorted out our stupid juvenile fighting.

SARAH. *(insistent)* Did you ever tell him you loved him?

(Pause. PHIL does not reply.)

Listen to me, Phil. I think the time has come when you should think about—

PHIL. – I don't care what you think.

(Pause. SARAH tries again.)

SARAH. I think the time has come when you should think about getting some help. You're not coping—

PHIL. – I don't need any help—

SARAH. – coping with it, Phil! You're not coping with it!

PHIL. I'm coping with it! I'm coping with it in my own way!

SARAH. It's not healthy!

PHIL. Who says?

SARAH. Anybody! Anybody would say!

PHIL. So what should I do then, Sarah? Define "healthy"! What should I be doing, according to your rule book? I know! How about I put on Joe's favourite song and dance around to it?

SARAH. Phil, stop it. You know very well what I mean. You need to talk to someone.

PHIL. I need to talk to Joe.

(*Pause.* **SARAH** *is at a loss,* **PHIL** *still angry.*)

Come on then. Where do I turn? Who do you suggest I should I talk to?

SARAH. A professional! Someone who—

PHIL. – no!—

SARAH. – someone who can help you!

PHIL. I am not going to pay out a hundred quid an hour, to listen to some woman in suede loafers, talking shite.

SARAH. Well then, listen to me instead!

(**PHIL** *laughs bitterly.*)

Why is that funny? We were married, Phil, we had Joe together! Who's better qualified than I am?

PHIL. And who was the first domino in the line?

(*Pause.* **SARAH** *is hurt by* **PHIL**'s *comment, but he is not deterred.*)

You, Sarah. You and that walking steroid.

SARAH. That is a nasty thing to say. And it isn't true.

(*Pause.* **SARAH** *speaks quietly.*)

Kids Joe's age are difficult, Phil. Do you honestly think it would have been different with you there?

PHIL. Yes.

SARAH. Do you?

PHIL. Yes! I honestly think it would.

SARAH. You're in no mood to think rationally.

PHIL. I've found him.

SARAH. *(not listening)* I mean, you refuse to acknowledge your part in all this. You come down here every day – why? How can you bear it?

PHIL. I've found him.

(pause)

SARAH. *(quietly)* What?

PHIL. I've found him!

(SARAH stares at him. Encouraged, he carries on.)

He was here, playing football!

SARAH. *(bewildered)* But we already knew that.

PHIL. I know! I know we did! But you all thought he'd gone. I was the one who kept coming back, because I knew he'd still be here, and I knew one day he'd show his face. And he has. He has. I was the one. Not you. Not Glenn. Me.

(Pause. SARAH is defeated.)

SARAH. Phil, you have to stop this.

PHIL. *(softly)* I can't.

SARAH. You mustn't come here again! It's not good, it's not right! You have to stay away!

PHIL. *(louder)* I can't!

(Pause. SARAH is now weeping quietly. She sits on the bench.)

SARAH. I've tried climbing over this, crawling under it. But I can't. Every day, I wake up, and for a few seconds everything's normal, and then it's there. I know I've got to go through it, but I don't know. I don't know how I'm going to get through. I can't rely on Glenn, not for this. I need you, Phil. But you…you keep coming here…and I don't know how I'm supposed to… You're not the only one, Phil, can't you see that?

*(Pause. For a second or two, **PHIL** seems to have taken in what she has said, but then–)*

PHIL. I've found him.

*(**SARAH** looks at him and he speaks eagerly, trying to make her understand.)*

He came to me! You only missed him by a few seconds! I told you, didn't I? I told you he was still here!

SARAH. *(softly)* You have to stop this.

PHIL. Just listen. Keep quiet, and he'll come back.

SARAH. You haven't listened to a bloody word I've said!

PHIL. Look, just wait with me for a minute, will you? – he'll come back!

(He calls off.)

Joe! Your mum's here, mate!... *(to **SARAH**)* Bear with me. Listen.

SARAH. I am not going along with this, Phil. Either you get some help, or I don't see you again.

*(**PHIL** does not turn round.)*

You know, you're starting to frighten me.... Phil!

*(**PHIL** flaps his hand at her to silence her, still looking off.)*

Get some help. Get some proper help. And then call me.

*(**SARAH** exits. **PHIL** waits, hoping **JOE** will reappear. Nothing happens.)*

PHIL. "As I was walking up the stair... I met a man who wasn't there."

(pause)

"He wasn't there again today. I wish that he would go away."

(Pause. He looks around him)

Joe?

(Nothing happens.)

Your mum thinks I'm imagining all this. She thinks it's all here. (*He taps his head.*) But now... I find it harder to imagine you were ever actually around. With your "yeah, right"...your "aw, Dad!" That roll of your eyes that always drove me mad. Your feet up on the dashboard of my car. I can still feel the heavy, floppy weight of you, in your babygro, like a little bean bag, asleep on my chest while I watched the football. I can smell your hair. I can hear your funny snuffly breathing. I can see the triumph on your face when you took your first standing-up pee. The concentration when you used to sit on the edge of the bath, watching me shave.

I anticipated danger, all the time, when you were little. All the things that could happen to you. A bike accident. Choking. Drowning. Some arrogant dick in a four-by-four coming round a corner too fast. And I looked ahead, to when you'd become an adult. Drugs. Knives. Fast cars. I anticipated it. I stood guard. I tried to prepare, just in case. You feel so bloody helpless, Joe, sometimes. Being a father. You used to look at me and think I could put anything right. And most of the time I could. But there was always this little voice inside whispering "Wait....wait." And then a stranger came along and took you away from me. And I feel as if I made it happen. Willed it to happen.

I held you in my arms when you were less than five minutes old, Joe. And I swore... I swore...that no harm would ever come to you on my watch. And then I let you down. Something came along that I couldn't save you from.

(*Pause.* **PHIL** *stands.*)

I'll be back tomorrow.

(*As* **PHIL** *walks to the exit, the ball comes onto the stage again and* **PHIL** *picks it up, joy and hope back on his face. He starts to look around for* **JOE**. *Unseen by him,* **JOE** *enters and sits on the bench.*)

JOE. Mum thinks you're a retard.

(**PHIL** *closes his eyes in relief.*)

PHIL. Tell me what happened, Joe.

JOE. The police told you what happened.

PHIL. I want to hear it from you.

JOE. It happened like they said it happened. The bloke who did it, he was on something.

(**PHIL** *walks to the bushes, building up to anger, finishing up behind the bench.*)

PHIL. He was hiding behind those bushes.

JOE. Are you asking me or telling me?

PHIL. *(with deceptive calm)* And you were here on your own playing football.

JOE. I didn't know he was there.

(**PHIL** *turns on* **JOE**, *furious, shouting, so loudly that a startled* **JOE** *jumps off the bench.*)

PHIL. What were you thinking, Joe? What the hell were you doing? You... *(stumbling over his words for a moment in anger and frustration)* What were you doing? How many times have I told you—?

JOE. – yeah yeah, look both ways before you cross the road, don't put a metal knife in the toaster, don't swim after a big meal... You told me. You did the dad thing. Don't take it on.

(*Pause.* **JOE** *sits back down.*)

You can't keep coming back here.

(**PHIL** *sits next to him, not looking at him.*)

PHIL. I took you for granted. Because you wound me up, you drove me insane. I know it's natural, I know you can't like your kids all the time. But now...because of what happened... I hate myself for every sharp word I ever said to you.

JOE. You could be a bit of a dick.

(**PHIL** *smiles at* **JOE**, *who grins back.*)

PHIL. I'd rant and I'd rave, I'd tell your mother she'd given birth to an arrogant little shit. And then I'd go into your room and watch you sleeping, and all that irritation blew away like fairy dust.

SARAH. *(off)* Phil...

(Enter **SARAH**. *She can't see* **JOE**.*)*

I'm sorry.

*(***PHIL** *holds up a hand.)*

What?

PHIL. He's here.

*(***SARAH** *shakes her head sadly. She is standing very close to* **JOE**.*)*

He's right next to you.

(For a moment, **SARAH** *is caught up in the fantasy. Then she recovers.)*

SARAH. *(moving away from* **JOE**) What did I just say?

PHIL. Colder.

SARAH. What?

PHIL. You're getting colder. *(She turns back to him.)* Warmer.

SARAH. Come with me now. Let's go—

PHIL. – warmer...

SARAH. Look. You're going to come with me now, to the café.

*(***PHIL** *is grinning at* **JOE**, *who is finding the whole thing funny.)*

Are you listening to me? We're going to get some hot chocolate and we're going to talk.

JOE. Go with her, Dad.

PHIL. Just a minute, Joe.

*(***SARAH** *is startled for a second, then impatient.)*

SARAH. Phil, please. Stop it!

(Something suddenly occurs to her.)

Are you doing this to try and get me back?

(**PHIL** *stares at her in disbelief.*)

Are you? Because if you are, it's not the way. You haven't seen Joe, of course you haven't – you're doing it to try and get me interested in you again. You're sad, Phil; you're lonely and you're sad, and you can't see how much you're hurting me with this fantasy! We are not getting back together. Accept that.

(*pause*)

PHIL. Well, I'm flattered.

SARAH. Look –

PHIL. No no – I'm flattered, Sarah. I love the fact that I live in your imagination as this pathetic lonely tosser who's pretending to see his dead son to get back into his ex wife's bed.

(*During their argument,* **JOE** *– who obviously has had to hear this a lot – resignedly walks out.*)

Do you really think you're that special?

SARAH. What would you say to me, Phil?

PHIL. Do you really think you're that special?

SARAH. What would you say to me, if this were the other way round? You've never believed in ghosts, you've always said it's a load of rubbish!

PHIL. It's not a ghost! It's Joe! He's right here!

(**PHIL** *looks triumphantly towards where* **JOE** *was standing – when he realises he's gone, he sinks onto the bench and puts his head in his hands.* **SARAH** *responds to his defeat, goes over to him and sits down.*)

SARAH. Sometimes I think I've seen him too. I see a boy with Joe's walk, Joe's smile. And I can't breathe for a minute. And then I look again, and it isn't him. Of course it isn't him.

(*pause*)

PHIL. I can't let him go.

SARAH. You don't have to. You can talk to me about him. As much as you like.

PHIL. What about Mr Universe? *(He smiles sadly.)* Joe calls him Glenda.

SARAH. Joe was ours. Yours and mine. Glenn can never compete with that. You and I wanted him, you and I made him. We loved him. And we can help each other through this. All we have to do is talk to each other.

*(At last, **PHIL** turns to her and smiles.)*

PHIL. We weren't very good at that, in the end.

(They smile at each other – we see their shared history, that whatever happens now, they had a child together and lost him, and they are bound by this, whether or not they want to be.)

SARAH. Come on. Let's get that hot chocolate.

(She starts to leave.)

PHIL. I was just thinking about when he was little.

SARAH. Not now, Phil. *(She looks around and shivers.)* I hate this place.

PHIL. You said I could talk about him.

SARAH. But not here. Don't come back here again, Phil. If you want to believe Joe's still around, then imagine him in the places where he was happy.

PHIL. Do you remember how he used to jump on me when he wanted me to carry him?

*(**SARAH** smiles, remembering.)*

SARAH. He'd run up behind you and jump on your back, like a little monkey.

PHIL. Sometimes he'd stay there and fall asleep. Remember?

SARAH. I remember everything, Phil. Please, never ever think I don't. That's what keeps me sane. And the trial's coming up…we'll go together. They'll put that man away, we'll watch them put him away.

(pause)

You don't get over it, you know, you just get better at it. And some days I'll enjoy a meal. Enjoy hearing a song that Joe liked. Or laugh at something, without feeling guilty. And then when I'm not thinking, it comes back, and it hits me as hard as it did when the police came to the door. That's what I need you to understand. I'm it, Phil. I'm the one. I'm the one who knows. Stop fighting me, stop blaming me.

PHIL. You were right, you know.

SARAH. Was I?... About what?

PHIL. I never told him I loved him.

SARAH. I shouldn't have said that to you. I was wrong. I'm sorry.

PHIL. It never occurred to me.

*(He looks at **SARAH**, as if only just realising what he is saying.)*

I never said I loved him. I just... I suppose I just thought he knew.

(He shakes his head, puzzled, defeated.)

I thought I'd found him. I really thought...

SARAH. *(kindly)* I know, love. I know you did.

PHIL. I thought I'd found him.

*(Pause. **SARAH** waits.)*

If I could touch him again, just once... I'd give anything. Just once. To touch him. To hear his voice... What does it...? If all of this is in my head, Sarah... if he's really gone from me...what does that leave me with?

SARAH. Find a place for him. You can keep loving him forever. Moving on doesn't mean leaving Joe behind, Phil.

*(**SARAH** moves to the exit.)*

Come on now. You can pay for the hot chocolate, I'll buy the cake.

(**SARAH** *exits.*)

(*music*)

(**PHIL** *stays where he is for a while, looking around him. After a while, he stands, taking one last look around, mentally giving up on his quest to find* **JOE**.)

(*As he is standing there* **JOE** *enters from behind* **PHIL**, *running to him and jumping on his back, putting his arms round his shoulders.* **PHIL** *stops and closes his eyes.* **JOE** *hugs him tightly.*)

(*After a moment,* **JOE** *slides off* **PHIL**'s *back, takes a step back and smiles as* **PHIL** *turns to him. He holds out his hand, but* **PHIL** *looks straight through him. Because his mind has been put at rest, he can no longer 'see' him.*)

(**JOE** *watches sadly as at last we see relief and acceptance on* **PHIL**'s *face. He exits purposefully.*)

(**JOE** *runs after him, and stops just before he gets to the wings. He stands for a moment, totally lost. Then he exits, the opposite way to* **PHIL**.)

(*Lights down, spot on.*)

(*After a few beats, the football rolls onto the stage into the spot.*)

Lightning Source UK Ltd.
Milton Keynes UK
UKOW04f0926190816

281048UK00008B/94/P